CONFLICT AT WORK

G.R.A.C.E. Your Way to Resolution

BY MICHELLE MAJORS

Copyright © 2024 by Dr. Michelle Majors

All rights reserved. No part of this book may be reproduced or used in any manner without written permission of the copyright owner except for the use of brief, cited quotations in a book review. For more information, contact: info@majorsleadership.com.

Dedication:

To Michele Storms of ACLU of Washington and Merf Ehman of Columbia Legal Services—leaders who exemplify the courage to bring their full humanity to their leadership, their decision-making, and conflict. Thank you for choosing to step into the danger of vulnerability.
You are brave.

Table of Contents

DISCLAIMER 1

MESSAGE FROM 3

OVERVIEW 5

UNIQUE CONFLICT DYNAMICS IN NONPROFITS 27

THE G.R.A.C.E. MODEL - The Alternative to the DEI Industrial Complex 37

G -GRACE 49

R -REFLECTION 59

A -ACCOUNTABILITY 69

C -CHOOSING THE RIGHT PATH FOR REPAIR 81

E - EVALUATE AND EVOLVE 105

REAL STORIES, REAL RESOLUTIONS 115

CONCLUSION 125

DISCLAIMER

The information provided in this book is intended for general informational purposes only and is not a substitute for professional legal advice or guidance. The author has made reasonable efforts to ensure the accuracy and completeness of the content, but makes no representations or warranties of any kind, express or implied, about the accuracy, suitability, or reliability of the information contained herein. Restorative conflict practices and principles may vary based on specific cases and other factors. Readers are advised to consult with qualified legal professionals or relevant authorities before applying any information or recommendations from this book to specific situations. The author, publisher, and distributor disclaim any liability for any loss, damage, or injury caused or alleged to
be caused, directly or indirectly, by the use or reliance on the information provided in this book.

Additionally, conflict involves complex human interactions and emotions, and outcomes may vary depending on individual circumstances. The author does not assume responsibility for the outcomes, consequences, or results of applying restorative conflict approaches discussed in this book. Readers are encouraged to exercise their judgment and discretion when implementing these practices.

By reading this book, you acknowledge that the author and all associated parties are not liable for any negative consequences that may arise from the application of restorative conflict concepts and methods presented within these pages.

MESSAGE FROM
THE CEO

Conflict is a natural component of any setting as rich and varied as the workplace. The pressing question we face is how to transform conflict from a disruptive force into a constructive one. How do we navigate disagreements with a dedication to mutual understanding and collective well-being? Conflict becomes restorative when we approach it with the aim of achieving clarity and perspective, not to point fingers or impose penalties.

In envisioning organizations, it's vital to see them not just as engines of productivity but as communities where every individual's story, viewpoint, and life experience is respected. To embrace grace is to recognize the inherent worth of every person and the transformative power of shared recovery. With grace at the forefront of conflict resolution, we can heal tensions, learn from our interactions, and foster a workplace where each member can flourish.

Let's adopt grace as our guiding principle, shaping workplaces where empathy and personal growth are interlaced, paving the way for enduring, positive transformation.

Dr. Michelle Majors

MLG
MAJORS LEADERSHIP GROUP

OVERVIEW

First, Restorative Justice Defined

Since this book centers on restorative conflict, it's important to also touch on its origins of restorative justice. I'll provide a high-level overview to give you a sense of where these concepts come from and how they've shaped our understanding of resolving conflicts in a more healing and positive way.

Restorative justice is a transformative approach to conflict resolution and justice that places a strong emphasis on healing, accountability, and community engagement. Unlike traditional punitive models, restorative justice seeks to address the harm caused by an offense by involving all stakeholders in a process of dialogue, understanding, and repair.

Overview

Historical Background: The roots of restorative justice can be traced back to Indigenous cultures and ancient practices of community-based justice. The principles of healing, restoration, and community involvement were embedded in traditional methods of conflict resolution and reconciliation in many societies around the world. In the modern context, restorative justice gained recognition and prominence in the late 20th century as a response to the limitations and shortcomings of the prevailing punitive justice system. The restorative justice movement emerged as a powerful alternative, offering a more holistic and inclusive approach to addressing crime, conflict, and harm.

By centering on the needs of victims, offenders, and the community, restorative justice aims to restore relationships, promote reconciliation, and build stronger, more resilient communities.

Restorative Conflict

Having explored the origins and principles of restorative justice, we now shift our focus to the concept of restorative conflict, the theme of this book, emphasizing its critical role in fostering a harmonious workplace environment.

Overview

Conflict is an inevitable part of the human experience, particularly in environments rich in diversity like the workplace. The big question is: How can we turn conflicts into something good and helpful? How do we approach this conflict with a commitment to everyone being restored and whole? Conflict resolution becomes restorative when it is approached with the intent to gain clarity and perspective between each other, rather than to assign blame or administer punitive measures.

By focusing on the root causes of conflict and working collaboratively towards solutions that benefit everyone, restorative conflict transforms disputes into opportunities for growth, learning, and strengthening bonds within the community or workplace.

Restorative conflict between two or more people in the workplace centers around several key elements that are essential to not only addressing disputes but also in nurturing a culture of mutual respect, understanding, and long-term positive change within organizations.

> **Voluntary Participation/Willing Spirit:** All parties involved must choose to engage in the restorative process willingly, without coercion, to ensure a genuine and constructive dialogue, providing an opportunity for them to share their experiences, express their emotions, and gain a deeper understanding of the impact of the offense.

Overview

- **Self-Reflection:** Through self-reflection, individuals can better understand their own emotions and perspectives, as well as those of others involved in the conflict. This fosters empathy, enabling parties to recognize the impact of their actions and to consider the feelings and needs of others. By understanding their own motivations and behaviors, individuals are better equipped to express themselves clearly and listen actively to others.

- **Accountability:** The individual who caused the harm acknowledges their role in the conflict, accepts responsibility for their actions, and understands how those actions have affected others. This accountability is crucial for moving towards resolution and healing. At this point, the person harmed may also look to see where they may have contributed to the conflict.

- **Collaborative Problem-Solving:** With a foundation of self- awareness, parties are also more likely to work together effectively to identify shared solutions that address the needs and concerns of all parties moving forward.

The Costs of Being Punitive

These days, when things go south—someone breaks a rule, crosses a line, or causes harm—our go-to reaction is to point fingers and demand conflict, the kind that often ends with a penalty. This traditional take, where we're doling out punishments left and right, boils down to a simple formula: do the crime, pay the time (or the fine). It's a method steeped in the idea of making those who cause harm "pay their dues" to society. This approach places a heavy focus on retribution and keeping the peace but not so much on healing the rifts caused or considering what led to the behavior in the first place. And, if we're being honest, this mindset stems from a fundamental human craving for assigning blame rather than promoting understanding and forgiveness.

This brings us to a critical point. Let's take a closer look at where the punitive approach has failed us and why it's time to think about changing our strategy.

- **Lack of Resolution for Underlying Issues:** Punitive approaches often fail to address the root causes of conflicts or misunderstandings. By focusing on punishment, these models may neglect the complex underlying factors that led to the conflict in the first place, such as systemic issues or personal circumstances.

Overview

- **Escalation of Resentment and Hostility:** Punitive measures can lead to increased resentment and hostility between the parties involved. The individual or group being punished may feel unjustly treated, leading to further antagonism rather than reconciliation.

- **Limited Opportunities for Learning and Growth:** By emphasizing punishment over constructive dialogue, the punitive model misses opportunities for individuals to learn from their mistakes, understand the impact of their actions, and develop empathy. Restorative models, in contrast, encourage learning and personal growth by engaging the parties in dialogue.

- **Cycle of Retaliation:** Punitive approaches can perpetuate a cycle of retaliation, where each action is met with a counteraction, escalating the conflict further rather than moving towards resolution.

- **Impacts on Community Cohesion:** In a community or organizational context, punitive approaches can damage relationships and undermine trust, leading to a fragmented community. This can be particularly

- detrimental in environments that rely on collaboration and mutual respect.

- **Inequity and Bias:** Punitive systems can disproportionately affect certain groups, leading to inequities. This is especially concerning in societal contexts where systemic biases may influence who is punished and how severely.

- **Costs and Resources:** Punitive measures, especially in legal settings, can be resource-intensive, diverting time and financial resources away from potentially more effective restorative or preventive measures.

- **Limited Effectiveness in Behavior Change:** Research suggests that punishment alone is often ineffective in achieving long-term behavioral change. Without addressing the motivations behind actions and facilitating a deeper understanding of the consequences, punitive approaches may not lead to the desired outcomes.

The Benefits of Being Restorative

Restorative conflict models, on the other hand, aim to address many of these limitations by focusing on dialogue, mutual understanding, and healing. It's like stepping into a world where, instead of defaulting to finding the bad guy and

Overview

making them regret it, we pause and lean into grace. Restorative conflict models are not about letting someone off the hook; they are about diving deep into the why and the how, mending what's broken, and, most importantly, doing it together.

It asks us to rethink deeply held beliefs about restoration and accountability. But, in doing so, it opens up a space where real healing is possible — not just in theory but in tangible ways that make our organizations stronger and more resilient. So, while the road to embracing a restorative approach might be less traveled, it's rich with the potential for genuine transformation and peace.

Punitive conflict has been the dominant paradigm for centuries. Its limitations have prompted calls for alternative approaches that prioritize healing, restoration, and community engagement.

Restorative conflict, for example, seeks to address these limitations by focusing on repairing harm, involving all stakeholders, promoting accountability, and offering opportunities for healing, growth, and community building.

Instead of focusing solely on punishment, restorative conflict aims to address the root causes of the conflict. It seeks to find resolutions that address the needs of all parties involved

Overview

and contribute to the well-being of other individuals affected indirectly, as well as the community.

Now, Let's Set the Foundation

Before diving into the implementation of a Restorative Conflict Model within your organization, it's crucial to establish a solid foundation. This groundwork involves a clear articulation of commitments and processes to address conflict effectively when it arises, alongside a keen awareness of the potential challenges you may encounter. Ensuring these elements are well-defined and understood is the first step toward fostering an environment where restorative practices can thrive. It sets a clear expectation for how conflicts are approached, emphasizing understanding, healing, and resolution over punishment or avoidance. This section aims to guide you through these foundational requirements, providing the insights and tools necessary for a successful transition to a more restorative conflict management approach.

Write it Down!

Putting restorative conflict commitments, practices, and policies into writing is important for organizations. Compare it to the significance of building a strong foundation for a skyscraper. A poor foundation will lead to an unstable building that, with time, is at risk of collapse. When we write down these promises, we create a clear map that everyone can follow.

Overview

This map helps everyone understand how to handle conflicts in a fair and consistent way. Just as we all agree on the rules of a game before playing, these written promises are the rules for resolving conflicts. These written promises become our guiding light when things get tough.

When there's a conflict, the written guidelines show everyone how to handle it. They ensure that we don't just react; I instead, we follow a path that's fair and clear.

Written policies show that everyone matters and is treated the same way. They also help new people understand how things work and what's expected when conflicts come up.

Now, let's think about what happens if these promises aren't written down. Without clear guidelines, different people might handle conflicts in different ways, causing confusion. It's like speaking different languages and not understanding each other.

In the absence of a clear reference, individuals might interpret the essence of restorative conflict differently, leading to unintentional missteps in conflict resolution attempts. This can undermine the very foundation of constructive dialogue and mutual understanding that restorative conflict aims to foster.

Overview

From a legal standpoint, the absence of written policies exposes the organization to vulnerabilities. In scenarios where conflicts escalate and legal actions are pursued, a lack of documented policies can cast doubt on the organization's commitment to addressing conflicts with restorative conflict principles.

In conclusion, the act of committing restorative conflict principles, practices, and policies to writing is pivotal for organizations seeking to navigate conflicts constructively. Written documentation lays the groundwork for a harmonious, accountable, and transparent approach to conflict resolution. It strengthens an organization's culture, builds trust, and ensures that the pursuit of resolution is founded on a steadfast commitment to restorative conflict values.

The Role of Leadership

Leadership plays a crucial role in promoting restorative conflict within an organization or community. Here are some key takeaways outlining ways leaders can contribute to the advancement of restorative conflict:

1. **Setting the Vision and Values:** Leaders have the responsibility to articulate a clear vision and values that align with restorative conflict principles. They can communicate the importance of fostering a culture of

healing, accountability, and community engagement. By consistently highlighting these values and integrating them into the organization's or community's mission, leaders create a foundation for restorative practices to thrive.

2. **Modeling Restorative Behavior:** Leaders serve as role models for others to follow. They can demonstrate restorative behavior by actively engaging in restorative practices themselves. This includes taking responsibility for their actions, seeking reconciliation, and showing empathy and understanding towards others. By modeling restorative behavior, leaders inspire and encourage others to adopt similar practices and attitudes.

3. **Providing Resources and Training:** Leaders can allocate resources, such as funding and personnel, to support the implementation of restorative conflict practices. They can ensure that there are appropriate training programs and resources available to help individuals understand and effectively engage in restorative processes. By investing in the necessary tools and training, leaders demonstrate their commitment to promoting restorative conflict within the organization or community.

4. **Encouraging Collaboration and Dialogue:** Leaders play a critical role in fostering collaboration and dialogue among stakeholders. They can create opportunities for individuals to come together, share their perspectives, and engage in meaningful conversations. By facilitating open and inclusive communication, leaders encourage the exchange of ideas, the building of relationships, and the resolution of conflicts through restorative means.

5. **Addressing Systemic Issues:** Leaders have the power to address systemic issues that may hinder the implementation of restorative conflict. They can evaluate existing policies, procedures, and structures within the organization or community and identify areas where change is needed. By taking proactive steps to address systemic barriers, leaders create an environment that supports and sustains restorative practices.

6. **Celebrating and Recognizing Restorative Efforts:** Leaders can acknowledge and celebrate individuals and groups who demonstrate a commitment to restorative conflict. By publicly recognizing and appreciating their efforts, leaders reinforce the importance of restorative practices and motivate others to engage in similar actions. This recognition can be in the form of rewards, praise, or highlighting success stories that exemplify the positive impact of restorative conflict.

to engage in similar actions. This recognition can be in the form of rewards, praise, or highlighting success stories that exemplify the positive impact of restorative conflict.

7. **Advocating for Restorative Conflict:** Leaders have a platform and influence that can be used to advocate for restorative conflict on a broader scale. They can engage with policymakers, community leaders, and other stakeholders to promote the adoption and implementation of restorative practices. By using their voices to advocate for restorative conflict principles and values, leaders contribute to the advancement of restorative conflict within society.

Challenges to Implementing the Restorative Conflict Model

When implementing restorative conflict practices in the workplace, several barriers and areas of resistance may arise. It's important to anticipate and address these challenges to ensure successful integration. Here are some common barriers and areas of resistance:

1. **Lack of Awareness and Understanding:** One significant barrier is the lack of awareness and understanding of restorative conflict principles and practices. Some individuals may be unfamiliar with the concept or skeptical about its effectiveness.

Overcoming Lack of Awareness and Understanding:

Educating employees about the benefits and rationale behind restorative conflict can help overcome this barrier. Providing training sessions, sharing success stories, and offering clear explanations of how restorative conflict can address conflicts and promote a positive work environment are important steps to build understanding and buy-in.

Creating a safe and inclusive environment is crucial. This includes fostering active listening, empathy, and respect. Addressing power imbalances by promoting equitable participation and decision-making is essential. Clear policies against retaliation or retribution for participating in restorative processes should be established. By creating an environment that values and supports restorative conflict, employees will feel more encouraged to engage and overcome their resistance.

A gradual implementation approach can also be effective. Starting with small pilot projects, specific teams, or departments allows for learning, adjustment, and demonstrating success to gain broader acceptance and support across the organization. Gradual implementation also provides an opportunity to identify and address any challenges or barriers early on.

2. **Resistance to Change:** Change can be met with resistance, particularly if individuals are accustomed to more traditional punitive approaches or have been involved in conflicts that were not resolved restoratively in the past. People may resist the shift to restorative conflict due to fear of the unknown, concerns about losing control, or skepticism about its impact.

Overcoming Resistance to Change:

Effective change management strategies, including clear communication, involvement of key stakeholders, and addressing concerns and misconceptions, can help overcome this resistance. Clear communication is crucial in addressing resistance and concerns. Organizations should clearly communicate the purpose, goals, and expected outcomes of implementing restorative conflict.

Transparency about the process and addressing any misconceptions or fears are important. Regular and open dialogue with employees should be encouraged, allowing them to express their thoughts, concerns, and questions. Emphasizing the positive impact that restorative conflict can have on workplace relationships, conflict resolution, and the overall organizational culture helps employees understand its value.

3. **Power Imbalances and Organizational Culture:** Existing power imbalances and an organizational culture that favors hierarchical decision-making can create obstacles to implementing restorative conflict. If power dynamics and authoritarian structures are deeply ingrained, it may be difficult to establish an environment that values open dialogue, shared decision-making, and equal participation.

Overcoming Power Imbalances and Organizational Culture:

Explicitly addressing power imbalances, promoting transparency, and encouraging collaboration can help overcome this barrier. Leaders must model the behaviors they want to see and foster a culture of trust, respect, and empowerment.

Leadership support and modeling are vital to overcoming challenges. Leaders should actively advocate for restorative practices, model restorative behaviors, and reinforce the principles of fairness, empathy, and accountability. When employees see leaders embracing restorative conflict, they are more likely to feel supported and motivated to participate.

4. **Fear of Accountability and Vulnerability:** Restorative conflict requires individuals to take accountability for their actions, engage in open dialogue, and express vulnerability. Some employees may be uncomfortable with these aspects, fearing potential consequences or exposure of their weaknesses. It's important to create a safe and non-judgmental space where individuals feel supported in their journey towards growth and understanding. Building trust and emphasizing the restorative nature of the process can help alleviate these concerns.

Overcoming Fear of Accountability and Vulnerability:

It's important to create a supportive environment that normalizes these feelings as part of the growth process. Begin by setting clear expectations for accountability and modeling vulnerability from the top leadership levels. Establish trust through consistent and fair practices, and reassure individuals that the intent is not to shame or punish, but to learn and improve. Provide training on constructive feedback and active listening to foster empathy and understanding. Incorporate regular reflective practices that encourage personal responsibility and self-awareness. Celebrate successes and acknowledge the courage it takes to be accountable and vulnerable. By doing so, you'll cultivate a culture where individuals feel safe to own their actions and open up about their challenges.

In conclusion, the power of healing and restoration in the workplace through restorative conflict practices cannot be understated. By embracing a restorative approach, organizations can transform conflicts into learning experiences, repair relationships, and create a culture of trust, empathy, and accountability. Restorative conflict offers a path to address harm and conflicts in a way that promotes understanding, growth, and healing for all individuals involved.

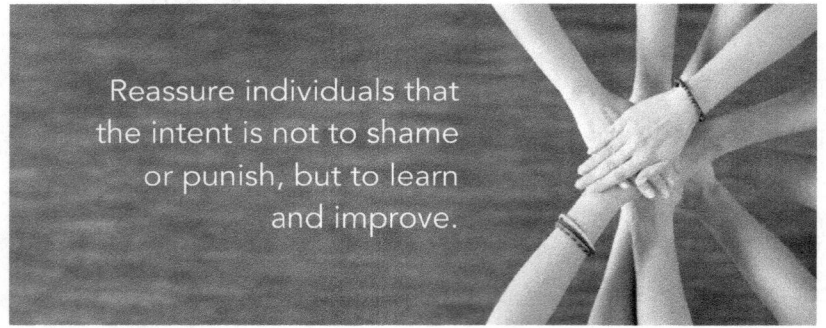

Overview

Reflection Questions:

1. How do the principles of restorative justice align with or differ from the traditional punitive approaches to conflict resolution that you have experienced in your personal or professional life?
2. In what ways can implementing restorative conflict practices in your workplace or community foster a more inclusive and empathetic environment?
3. What steps can you personally take to promote accountability, empathy, and collaborative problem-solving in conflicts you encounter?

Overview

UNIQUE CONFLICT DYNAMICS IN NONPFROFITS

In the realm of nonprofits, conflict takes on unique contours. At the intersection of individual activism and organizational accountability, staff members who are often also community representatives grapple with balancing personal convictions with collective responsibilities. The push and pull between passion for social justice and the pragmatism of operational mandates gives rise to distinctive challenges. Addressing these issues necessitates a nuanced approach, acknowledging the passionate activism that employees bring to the table while also considering the organization's broader duties to stakeholders.

UNIQUE CONFLICT DYNAMICS IN NONPROFITS

To fully grasp the scope of these challenges, it is essential to delve into the specific aspects that fuel tensions and disagreements. Here are the most significant conflict dynamics I've observed:

First, navigating the delicate balance between individual activism and organizational constraints presents a unique challenge in the nonprofit sector. As organizations strive for diversity, they often attract individuals deeply connected to the communities they serve, individuals who are passionate about being change makers and activists. These individuals may bring a grassroots approach to activism, advocating for bold stances on social justice issues. However, the nonprofit, as a business entity, must also remain accountable to a broader set of stakeholders, including board members, donors, and partners. This dual commitment can lead to conflicts when staff members feel that the organization's actions are not fully aligned with the values it publicly espouses.

The tension arises when personal values of activism clash with the organization's strategic objectives and responsibilities. For instance, a staff member might argue that the nonprofit is not "walking the walk," claiming a discrepancy between its proclaimed progressive stance and its actual practices. This perception of misalignment can foster a sense of disillusionment and can lead to contentious discussions about the organization's authenticity and commitment to its values.

The heart of the issue often lies in nonprofit leaders' reluctance to openly discuss the organization's limitations. Out of fear of rejecting proposals or appearing uncommitted to the cause, leaders may avoid honest conversations about the organization's capacity, barriers, and the practical constraints of staff expectations. To bridge this gap, nonprofit leaders need to foster an environment of transparent communication, where real dialogue about the organization's capabilities and limitations is encouraged, helping to align staff expectations with the organization's operational realities.

Secondly, there is a unique thing that happens when *staff* from marginalized groups are serving and protecting the rights of *community members* from marginalized groups.

Individuals from marginalized communities serving in roles that cater to similar groups bring a deep level of empathy and understanding to their work. Their lived experiences enable them to connect with and understand the challenges faced by the communities they serve, fostering a deep sense of trust and rapport. However, this close identification with the struggles of their clients can also lead to an emotional burden. Service providers may find themselves reliving their own traumas and adversities through the experiences of those they assist, a dynamic that can be both emotionally draining and psychologically taxing. This intense emotional engagement can lead to compassion fatigue, affecting their well-being and potentially impacting their ability to serve effectively.

Compounding this, service providers from marginalized communities often grapple with internalized challenges, such as dealing with the effects of internalized oppression or navigating complex identity dynamics within their professional roles. These internal conflicts can strain professional interactions and decision-making, affecting the quality of service and potentially leading to workplace tensions. Furthermore, heightened expectations are placed on these individuals, presuming an inherent capability to fully understand and address all aspects of their clients' needs.

The representation of marginalized individuals in service roles, while beneficial for inclusivity, can inadvertently lead to tokenism. This occurs when individuals feel valued solely for their demographic background rather than their professional skills and contributions. This perception of tokenism can diminish job satisfaction and contribute to feelings of isolation and undervaluation.

The combination of emotional burden, internalized challenges, unrealistic expectations, and tokenism creates a complex web of factors that can fuel and perpetuate conflict within organizations serving marginalized communities. Addressing these issues requires a nuanced understanding and strategic organizational interventions to support staff effectively and mitigate the potential for conflict.

For leaders of color, this challenge is compounded by an additional layer of expectations. They may feel pressure to advocate for staff of color, reflecting a broader societal demand for solidarity based on shared racial or cultural experiences. This pressure can create a conflict for the leader, who must navigate between the organization's performance standards and the expectations of their team.

These leaders of color are frequently placed in a precarious position, having to choose between being perceived as the 'bad guy' for upholding standards and penalizing staff of color who may not meet performance goals, or facing their own superiors to justify any perceived lapses. It's a choice between rigorous accountability and the risk of being labeled unsupportive or even traitorous to their community. Such dynamics can lead to a tense environment where leaders of color bear the brunt of criticism for actions they take, no matter how justified.

Finally, in some cases there is an underlying belief among some staff members from marginalized communities that the organization owes them a certain level of consideration and support, given its mission to serve marginalized groups.

They may feel that the organization, professing to understand and advocate for marginalized individuals, should also recognize, and accommodate the unique challenges faced by its own marginalized staff. This perspective can lead to expectations of leniency or special treatment in organizational policies and practices, under the premise that understanding marginalized experiences extends to all aspects of the organization's operations.

When these expectations are not met, or if the organization fails to adequately acknowledge and address the specific needs of its marginalized employees, feelings of disillusionment and resentment can surface. This disconnect between staff expectations and organizational response can further contribute to the conflict landscape, challenging the organization's ability to maintain a cohesive, supportive, and effective working environment.

The dynamic of fear among leaders, particularly white leaders, in confronting staff members with a bold and clear social justice analysis, plays a significant role in perpetuating conflict within organizations. Leaders may hesitate to performance manage these staff members, driven by concerns of appearing oppressive or being intimidated by the staff's assertive voice and analysis. This reluctance to engage in direct communication and feedback results in issues being overlooked or unaddressed, allowing minor problems to escalate into significant organizational conflicts. When eventually confronted, staff members are often taken aback, voicing legitimate grievances like "you never told me this before," pointing to a lack of clear communication and accountability from the beginning.

To avoid this conflict, leaders need to cultivate an environment of open and honest dialogue, where feedback is provided consistently and constructively, regardless of the potential discomfort it may bring. Establishing clear expectations, performance metrics, and communication channels from the outset can help in mitigating misunderstandings and preemptively addressing issues. Leaders should also engage in self-reflection and seek training to overcome fears related to perceived oppression or conflict, thus enabling them to manage performance effectively and equitably. This approach not only reduces the likelihood of conflicts arising from unspoken grievances but also strengthens the organization's capacity to handle social justice issues with integrity and courage.

UNIQUE CONFLICT DYNAMICS IN NONPROFITS

Reflection Questions:

1. How do the dual commitments of personal activism and organizational accountability create unique challenges within your nonprofit, and what strategies can you implement to navigate these tensions effectively?
2. In what ways can the emotional burden and compassion fatigue experienced by staff from marginalized communities affect their work, and what support mechanisms can be put in place to mitigate these impacts?
3. How can your organization address the potential for tokenism and unrealistic expectations placed on staff from marginalized backgrounds, ensuring that their professional skills and contributions are fully recognized and valued?

UNIQUE CONFLICT DYNAMICS IN NONPROFITS

Enter the G.R.A.C.E. Model: The Answer to the DEI Industrial Complex

The G.R.A.C.E. Model for Conflict offers a profound shift in how we perceive and address conflicts. Beyond the typical methods of confrontation and suppression, G.R.A.C.E. encapsulates a holistic framework that not only acknowledges the presence of conflict but actively strives to harness its potential for growth, healing, and reconciliation. Comprising a series of interconnected principles, G.R.A.C.E. stands as an acronym, each letter representing a pivotal step toward resolving conflicts in a way that repairs the damage and strengthens relationships while fostering personal and communal well-being.

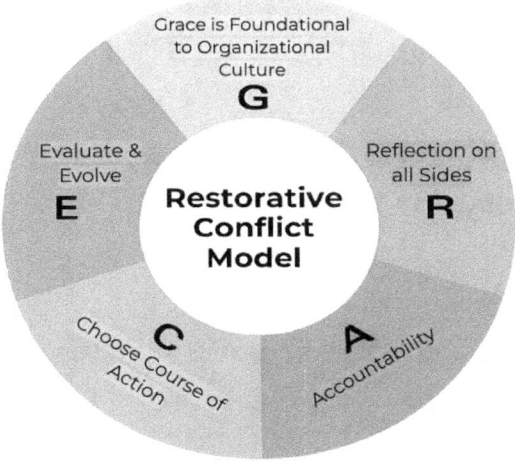

Enter the G.R.A.C.E. Model

From acknowledging the dynamics of conflict, to nurturing open dialogue and assuming accountability, to embarking on a path of healing and restoration, the G.R.A.C.E. Model offers a comprehensive roadmap. It empowers individuals, communities, and organizations to confront conflicts with a perspective that goes beyond winning or losing, advocating instead for a journey of mutual understanding, transformation, and renewed harmony.

To explore the G.R.A.C.E. Model's components, we will delve into the layers of recognizing conflict, self-reflection, accountability, communication, and the pursuit of healing. Each component contributes to the creation of a culture that values empathy, respect, and restoration— an approach that not only resolves conflicts but strengthens the bonds that hold us together.

The DEI Industrial Complex Has Failed Us

I used to call myself a DEI Consultant. I don't anymore. **I am a Difficult Conversation Strategist.**

This shift reflects my understanding that the core challenges in diversity, equity, and inclusion lie not merely in recognizing different identities, but in the crucial ability to communicate effectively across these varied identities. My focus now is on facilitating meaningful dialogue, bridging gaps, and fostering understanding in diverse work environments.

This shift also reflects my belief that the DEI Industrial Complex, while aiming to address systemic inequities, has fallen short of its intended goals especially in nonprofit settings.

To navigate this terrain, my clients and I have encountered four prevalent dynamics that challenge the very core of DEI work:

1. Mis-labeling Issues

While I believe that most, if not all, inequitable practices and work cultures have historical roots in inequality and injustice, there's a concerning trend of mislabeling things as equity issues when, in many cases, they're not. This includes attributing actions of others as racist, phobic, etc. when that simply isn't the case in some instances; or doing so with partial information. Such mislabeling not only undermines the integrity of genuine DEI efforts but also risks diverting attention from *real* and *deeper* systemic issues that perpetuate inequality and discrimination. It's crucial for organizations to maintain clarity and authenticity in their DEI initiatives, ensuring they address genuine issues while upholding principles of equity and inclusion.

Enter Grace: Rather than jumping to conclusions or attributing someone's actions to unconscious bias without full context, the Grace Equity® Model promotes a nuanced approach to addressing inequities. It encourages individuals to slow down and engage in dialogue, seek understanding, and refrain from making hasty judgments. Through intentional efforts to build bridges and foster genuine empathy, this model ensures that DEI initiatives remain grounded in clarity and authenticity. By upholding principles of equity and inclusion while addressing genuine issues, the Grace Equity® Model enables organizations to navigate complexities and work towards meaningful progress in creating more equitable and inclusive environments.

2. Tokenizing

Often, DEI efforts in nonprofits result in superficial diversity where individuals from marginalized groups are included merely for optics, rather than being valued for their unique perspectives and contributions. This perception of tokenism or performative activism within DEI initiatives can breed resentment and cynicism, hindering genuine progress towards unity.

To truly bridge divides, DEI efforts must prioritize building bridges of understanding, empathy, and collaboration, rather than inadvertently widening existing rifts.

Enter Grace: Rather than superficially including individuals from marginalized groups for the sake of optics, (G)race Equity® emphasizes the authentic valuing of diverse perspectives and contributions.

By shifting the focus from performative actions to genuine engagement and inclusion, (G)race Equity® fosters a culture of respect and appreciation for diverse voices. Rather than breeding resentment and cynicism, as tokenism often does, the (G)race Equity® Model promotes a sense of belonging and trust within organizations. Through intentional efforts to understand, empathize, and collaborate across differences, (G)race Equity® works towards dismantling barriers and building bridges that lead to true unity and progress.

3. Good/bad-right/wrong Dichotomies

The dichotomy of good/bad or right/wrong in the context of DEI work often sets a stage for oversimplification of complex human dynamics. This binary thinking can leave individuals feeling judged and categorized, fostering an environment of defensiveness rather than openness to growth and understanding.

People may feel compelled to perform 'correctness' rather than engage in authentic learning or dialogue, for fear of being labeled 'bad' or 'wrong' if they misspeak or misunderstand a concept. Such an atmosphere can inadvertently create barriers to genuine DEI efforts, as it can stifle the free exchange of ideas and inhibit the vulnerability necessary for meaningful change.

When individuals feel they are walking on a tightrope of judgment, the fear of making mistakes can override the intent to connect with others and participate in DEI initiatives, leading to resistance, surface-level compliance, or even total disengagement from the process.

Enter Grace: By intertwining grace with equity, we acknowledge that the journey toward inclusivity is paved with learning, unlearning, and relearning where missteps are met with hands that lift us up rather than punitive glares that push us down. Rather than trapping individuals in a cycle of judgment, Grace Equity pushes for a powerful yet compassionate approach to inclusion, recognizing our shared journey of continuous learning. This model fosters a spirit of collaborative resilience, inviting each person to contribute to an environment where every voice is valued not just in word but in action. It paves the way for sustainable change by transforming barriers into steppingstones towards a more empathetic and equitable organization.

4. Us Versus them & Problematic Power

DEI initiatives can tend toward an 'us versus them' mindset between staff and leadership, often fueled by embedded distrust stemming from historical inequities. But also fueled by the DEI Industrial Complex narrative that inherently perpetuates this mindset. The narrative itself demands an oppressor; it demands an enemy.

Positional Power: Despite outward professions of commitment to DEI work, leaders may find the challenges overwhelming internally, leading to a desire to slow down progress without admitting it. This lack of transparency can leave staff feeling gaslit and frustrated, as efforts are continually thwarted. Also, leaders may secretly resent staff empowerment, viewing it as a loss of control, and may label staff as entitled when they assert their rights or demand accountability.

Over time, leaders may grow weary of the pressure for transparency and accountability, resorting back to silencing resistance and reverting to hierarchical frameworks to regain perceived control.

Leaders, in their pivotal roles, can fuel a "them versus us" mentality through their own insecurities. These insecurities may not always be evident but can manifest as deep-seated fears that bleed into their leadership style. This fear can drive leaders to adopt defensive tactics and create strategies that inadvertently perpetuate division. In my experience, it's these profound insecurities that create obstacles that hindering leaders from effectively steering the DEI journey. Recognizing and addressing these fears is critical to dismantling barriers and fostering a culture of trust and collective growth.

Social Power: Meanwhile, I *have* seen staff behave in ways that range from a sense of entitlement to outright bullying. Whether under the guise of "speaking truth to power" or genuine intentions to foster inclusivity. To be clear, I believe that it is mission critical for staff to have the power and voice to demand transparency and accountability. When we can hold our leaders accountable, this is how we know we matter. However, in my experience, this demand is not always rooted in a desire to understand and collaborate and better the organization, but sometimes is simply a means to reclaim individual or collective power or control. This manifests in a myriad of ways including, hyper vigilance/critique of leadership's decisions, demand for information they are not entitled to, for example, wanting to know why a person of color was fired; and if they don't receive said information, they assume nefarious motives by leadership. Sometimes these calls to hold leadership accountable are more about deflecting from staff members that may be looking to *dodge their own personal accountability*. Or it's about deflecting from deeper organizational issues that staff may be benefiting from—like leadership being too afraid to performance-manage and provide growth feedback. This allows the staff member to escape accountability for performance.

Enter Grace: The Grace Equity® Model offers a transformative approach to address the 'us versus them' dynamic perpetuated by traditional DEI initiatives. By emphasizing grace and equity, this model tears down hierarchical barriers and brings interactions to a more human level. Rather than perpetuating divisions between staff and leadership, Grace Equity® fosters a culture of empathy, understanding, and collaboration. It encourages open dialogue and mutual respect, recognizing the inherent value of every individual's perspective and contribution. By transcending divisive dynamics and fostering a sense of shared purpose and belonging within the organization, Grace Equity® creates a space where hierarchy dissolves, and individuals connect on a deeply human level.

The Grace Equity® Model stands out as the definitive response to DEI's current challenges, offering a pragmatic and empathetic solution where others fall short. It systematically dismantles the harmful binaries of good/bad and right/wrong that alienate rather than unite, and it replaces quick judgments with a commitment to understanding and genuine dialogue. This model is a strategic ally in the quest for real inclusion, paving the way for an organizational culture that values clarity, authenticity, and shared accountability.

All this said, I want to take a moment to honor my clients and others who bravely engage in the work, fully aware that they will make mistakes and likely get beat up for it, yet they press on, embracing vulnerability as a step towards progress. They face embarrassment, engage in deep self-reflection, hold themselves accountable and put things right. As a conversation strategist, I have had the good fortune to support many such individuals. Equally inspiring are those who, having been on the receiving end of these missteps, respond with immense grace and understanding, recognizing the shared human endeavor to improve.

Despite these pockets of earnest effort, I maintain that the overarching DEI system is flawed, often doing more to divide us than to bring us together—and for this reason, I'm out. #SharkTank

Enter the G.R.A.C.E. Model

Reflection Questions:

1. How can integrating the principles of grace and accountability in the G.R.A.C.E. Model transform the way you perceive and address conflicts within your organization?
2. In what ways can self-reflection and mutual understanding, as emphasized in the G.R.A.C.E. Model, help in overcoming the challenges posed by the good/bad-right/wrong dichotomies in DEI work?
3. How can the G.R.A.C.E. Model help in addressing the 'us versus them' dynamics within your organization, and what steps can you take to promote a culture of empathy, collaboration, and shared purpose?

Enter the G.R.A.C.E. Model

G – GRACE

Photo by Alex Shute on Unsplash

What Does the Science Say

By now, you may have figured out that I lead with grace. In our society marked by so much division and discord, conversations across identities are more crucial than ever. Yet, these dialogues often evoke intense emotions, defensive reactions, and deep-seated misunderstandings. How can we navigate these turbulent waters and foster meaningful, productive discussions? The answer lies in a timeless, yet profoundly powerful principle: grace.

Grace is more than a simple act of kindness; it is a dynamic force that transforms interactions, builds bridges, and heals wounds. In the context of dialogue about our different identities, grace becomes an essential tool for fostering empathy, reducing defensiveness, and promoting

psychological safety. It enables us to approach these conversations with patience, understanding, and forgiveness, creating a space where genuine understanding and reconciliation can flourish.

Scientific research underscores the transformative power of grace when having challenging conversations across our differences. Studies have shown that environments characterized by psychological safety—where individuals feel safe to express their thoughts and emotions without fear of judgment—lead to more open and honest communication. This is crucial when discussing sensitive topics like race and racism, where fear of negative consequences can stifle true dialogue.

As we delve deeper into the science behind grace in dialogue about our different identities, we will uncover how this powerful principle can enhance conflict resolution, support healing and reconciliation, and encourage a growth mindset. By integrating grace into our conversations, we not only address the issues at hand but also lay the foundation for a more inclusive and compassionate society.

1. Promotes Psychological Safety

Research Findings: Psychological safety, a concept developed by Dr. Amy Edmondson, is crucial for open dialogue. It refers to an environment where individuals feel safe to take interpersonal risks, such as discussing sensitive topics like race and racism without fear of negative consequences.

Evidence: Studies have shown that psychological safety fosters open communication, trust, and mutual respect, which are essential for productive dialogues on race and racism (Edmondson, 1999; Carmeli et al., 2009).

2. Reduces Defensive Reactions

Research Findings: Conversations about race can trigger defensive reactions, especially among individuals who feel accused or blamed.

Practicing grace, which involves patience, understanding, and forgiveness, can help mitigate these defensive responses.

Evidence: Research by Dr. John Gottman has shown that grace and positive interactions can counteract the negative effects of defensiveness and create a more open and empathetic communication environment (Gottman & Silver, 1999).

3. Fosters Empathy and Understanding

Research Findings: Empathy is a critical component in discussions about race and racism. Graceful communication encourages individuals to listen actively and empathetically, fostering a deeper understanding of different perspectives.

Evidence: Neuroscientific studies have demonstrated that empathy activates specific brain regions associated with understanding and sharing the feelings of others, which can bridge divides and reduce racial biases (Decety & Cowell, 2014).

4. Enhances Conflict Resolution

Research Findings: Graceful communication strategies align with effective conflict resolution techniques, which emphasize the importance of addressing underlying needs and concerns rather than surface-level disagreements.

Evidence: Studies on conflict resolution, such as those by Morton Deutsch and Peter T. Coleman, highlight that approaches grounded in mutual respect, empathy, and grace lead to more sustainable and constructive outcomes in conflicts related to race and racism (Deutsch & Coleman, 2000).

5. Supports Healing and Reconciliation

Research Findings: Grace plays a significant role in healing and reconciliation processes. It allows for acknowledgment of past harms, the expression of remorse, and the possibility of forgiveness and moving forward.

Evidence: Research on restorative justice practices, which incorporate principles of grace, has shown positive effects in terms of reducing recidivism, fostering understanding, and promoting community healing (Braithwaite, 2002; Zehr, 2002).

6. Encourages Growth Mindset

Research Findings: A growth mindset, as developed by Dr. Carol Dweck, is essential for learning and change. Graceful interactions encourage individuals to view mistakes and misunderstandings as opportunities for growth rather than as failures.

Evidence: Studies have demonstrated that a growth mindset leads to increased resilience, openness to feedback, and a willingness to engage in difficult conversations, including those about race and racism (Dweck, 2006).

Practical Implications

Facilitation Techniques: Incorporating grace into dialogue facilitation techniques can create more inclusive and effective conversations. This includes setting ground rules that promote respectful listening, providing space for reflection, and encouraging compassionate responses.

Training and Education: Organizations can benefit from training programs that emphasize the role of grace in communication, helping employees develop the skills needed to navigate discussions about race and racism constructively.

Grace & Restorative Conflict

Grace is fundamental to the philosophy and practice of restorative conflict resolution for several reasons, deeply intertwining with its core principles of empathy, understanding, and reconciliation.

First, grace embodies the act of giving others the space to be imperfect. In the context of restorative conflict, it means approaching situations with an open heart and a willingness to forgive, even when the initial impulse may be to seek retribution or hold onto grievances. This is essential because conflicts often arise from misunderstandings, mistakes, or the actions of individuals acting under stress or out of ignorance. By leading with grace, parties in conflict are encouraged to move beyond the surface level of wrongdoing to understand the underlying causes of behavior. This understanding paves the way for genuine dialogue, healing, and the potential for transformation.

Secondly, grace is about extending compassion and empathy, even when it's challenging to do so. It requires seeing the humanity in everyone involved in a conflict, recognizing that each person has their own struggles, fears, and vulnerabilities. This perspective fosters a restorative environment where individuals feel seen, heard, and valued, which is critical for breaking down barriers and building trust. When people feel that their experiences and emotions are acknowledged, they are more likely to engage in open and honest communication, essential for resolving conflicts and restoring relationships.

Lastly, grace involves the willingness to relinquish both control and the desire for punishment, embracing instead a focus on healing and growth for all involved. It challenges the punitive model of conflict resolution, which often seeks to assign blame and administer punishment, rather than address the root causes of the conflict and work towards a solution that benefits everyone. By centering on grace, restorative conflict approaches emphasize accountability in a supportive manner, encouraging individuals to take responsibility for their actions and their impacts on others but doing so from a place of wanting to repair harm and make amends, rather than from a place of shame or guilt.

G-GRACE

Reflection Questions:

1. How can practicing grace in conversations about race and racism help create an environment of psychological safety within your organization or community?
2. In what ways can adopting a graceful approach to dialogue reduce defensive reactions and foster empathy among participants?
3. Reflect on a recent conversation about race or identity where tensions were high. How might incorporating the principles of grace—such as patience, understanding, and forgiveness—have altered the outcome of that dialogue?

G-GRACE

G-GRACE

G-GRACE

R – REFLECTION

Conflict often acts as a mirror, reflecting back to us the immediate disagreement and the shadows of unresolved traumas, past hurts, and deep-seated wounds. It's in these heated moments that our unexamined past can cloud our judgment, leading us to react based on old patterns rather than the present reality. Without taking the time for self-reflection, we risk allowing these echoes of the past to shape our perceptions and decisions, almost guaranteeing that assumptions and conclusions are drawn from outdated scripts. To navigate conflicts effectively, it's essential to pause and reflect, ensuring our responses are rooted in the here and now, and not in bygone chapters of our lives. Consider the **Conflict Reaction Sequence**. A Framework by Dr. Majors

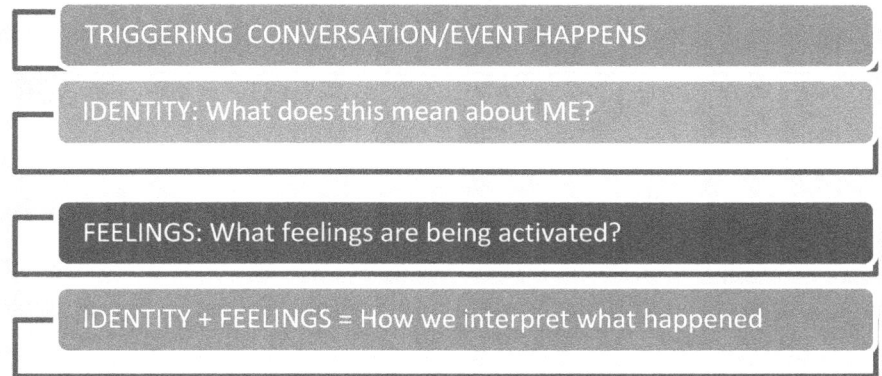

R – REFLECTION

Something Happens:

At the heart of difficult conversations lies the question of what exactly transpired. There's a problem though. It's not just about identifying the external actions but also *understanding how each person perceived and interpreted those actions*. This is where the conversation delves into the territory of differing viewpoints, memories, and interpretations, often revealing the gaps between intention and impact. By uncovering these layers, individuals can uncover how each party's unique understanding and misperceptions contribute to the tension, laying the groundwork for a more accurate and empathetic discussion.

From a deeper perspective, everyone carries a unique collection of past events, memories, and emotions that color their perception of the present conflict. Personal histories shape the lens through which people interpret actions, words, and intentions, often leading to a divergence of viewpoints. Adding to this, trauma and lingering wounds from previous conflicts or relationships can strongly influence one's understanding of events, as well as trigger emotional responses that may seem disproportionate to one's an outsider who has not lived that experience. An innocuous comment or passing statement might bring back past hurts and ramp up the current conflict's emotional intensity.

R – REFLECTION

Lived experiences act as lenses through which individuals interpret the world around them. Cultural backgrounds, upbringing, social conditioning, and personal triumphs all contribute to the unique way each person views conflict. These experiences can lead to assumptions, biases, or expectations that influence how individuals perceive what transpired.

Feelings and emotions are being activated:

Emotions often simmer beneath the surface during difficult conversations, shaping the way people react and respond. The "Feelings" conversation invites participants to acknowledge and express their emotions openly, going beyond the superficial "I'm fine" response and encouraging a deeper exploration of the emotional impact that the conflict has had on everyone.

By sharing these feelings, people can bridge the empathy gap and foster an environment of understanding through dialogue. This conversation acknowledges the human aspect of conflict, recognizing that emotions are a natural response and that addressing them directly can lead to a more authentic and productive conversation.

Emotions are not isolated reactions; they are a reflection of accumulated experiences, leading to nuanced responses that

R – REFLECTION

are influenced by the past. These intense emotions are windows into a person's struggle with the aftermath of trauma.

The emotional response in conflict is rarely about the other person. It is about the response that the other person has activated.

We assign meaning:
When we react to conflict, we're really asking how it makes us feel about *ourselves, our value, and our image.* Said another way instead of just seeing the disagreement as an isolated issue, we often interpret it as a reflection of our own worth or identity. This can make finding a solution more challenging because the conflict becomes entangled with our feelings about ourselves. If we recognize this habit, we can shift our focus back to the problem at hand, separate from our self-image.

If we could understand that conflicts don't define our worth, disagreements would look much simpler. We'd tackle them as just problems to solve, not battles that threaten our self-image.

This clarity would allow us to engage more calmly and creatively, focusing on solutions without the burden of personal offense or the need to defend our value as individuals.

For example, my husband and I used to have conflicts about his adult son visiting our home unannounced. His son would show up and stay for a day up to a week. I never knew when he was coming or when he was leaving. To be clear, he is a lovely young man I adore. But this habit drove me nuts! Coming from a background of homelessness, I am hyper-protective of my personal spaces, especially my home environment. I get agitated and feel disrespected when people pop in without the consideration of asking or at least letting me know.

Conversely, as a man who had his share of challenges with his father, my husband wanted to make sure that his sons were welcome to his home any time they chose.

R – REFLECTION

Needless to say, this became an ongoing issue because I felt that he wasn't honoring me and my needs as his wife, and he felt I wasn't honoring and being supportive of him as a father. We were deadlocked.

Until we could see that this wasn't about his son visiting, and understand it was about two adults reacting from their childhood traumas, this would have continued. Once we were both clear about the values that were driving us and the tender spots that we were protecting, we made some agreements where we both felt validated and satisfied.

In essence, our past wounds, traumas, and accumulated experiences strongly shape the lens through which we view conflicts. It's not solely about the surface-level disagreement; rather, these clashes are deeply influenced by how individuals *interpret and respond* to the conversation. Our history molds the emotional context we bring to conflicts, and our identity, a construct of personal narratives, guides our perception of the conflict's significance. Given this, we can now reflect on the conflict with more grace and accountability. Here are some guiding reflection questions to get started:

    a. **What Are My Emotions?** What emotions am I feeling right now? How might these emotions be influencing my thoughts and reactions?

R – REFLECTION

b. **What's My Goal?** What outcome am I hoping for in this conflict? Is my goal to understand, find a solution, or simply express my viewpoint?

c. **Am I Listening?** Am I actively listening to the other person's perspective, or am I focused solely on defending my own viewpoint?

d. **Am I Making Assumptions?** Am I making assumptions about the other person's intentions or feelings? How can I confirm or clarify those assumptions?

e. **Am I Taking Responsibility?** Am I taking responsibility for my own actions, feelings, and contributions to the conflict? Am I blaming the other person without acknowledging my role?

f. **What's the Desired Outcome?** What do I hope will be the outcome of this conflict resolution? How can I work toward that outcome?

R – REFLECTION

Another tool that may prove useful are the following reflections questions

What is the problem from my point of view?	What is the problem from their point of view?
What assumptions am I making that inform my perspective?	What assumptions might they be making that inform their perspective?
How have I contributed to the situation?	How have they contributed to the situation?
What feelings are coming up for me as I navigate this conflict?	What feelings might (have) come up for them as they navigate this conflict?
What do I fear this situation says about me?	What might they fear this situation says about them?

From JustLead Washington's Adaptation from "Difficult Conversations: How to Discuss What Matters Most."

R – REFLECTION

Reflection Questions:

1. How do your past experiences and unresolved traumas influence your emotional reactions and interpretations during conflicts?
2. In what ways can practicing self-reflection and identifying your own emotions help in reducing misunderstandings and fostering more productive dialogues during conflicts?
3. How can acknowledging and separating your personal identity and self-worth from the conflict at hand lead to more effective and solution-focused outcomes?

_____
_____
_____
_____
_____
_____
_____
_____
_____
_____
_____
_____

R – REFLECTION

A - ACCOUNTABILITY

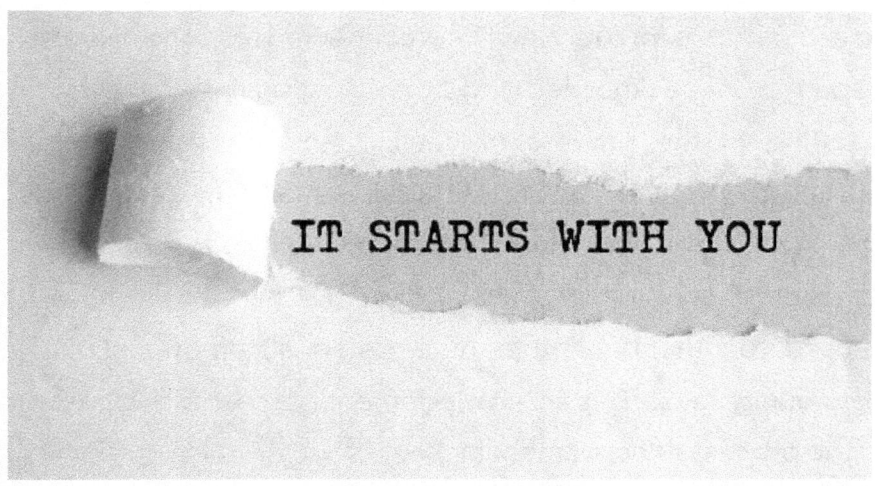

Resolving conflict means everyone involved needs to take a good look at their own actions. First, we've got ourselves – knowing our triggers and where they come from. Then, our colleagues can come together to support the right steps toward making amends. And let's not forget about leadership; those in charge need to lead by example, making sure everyone's on a path to sorting things out. In this chapter, we're breaking down how working on each level – individual, community, and leadership – is key to turning conflicts into opportunities to grow and come together.

Accountability of the Individual

At the heart of the restorative conflict framework, the individual is held accountable for a range of interconnected responsibilities that span from acknowledging their actions to actively participating in the process of healing and transformation. Specifically, the individual's accountability entails:

- **Acknowledging Harm:** The individual is responsible for recognizing and acknowledging the harm they have caused to others, whether on a personal, emotional, or community level. This acknowledgment is a crucial first step in the process of accountability.

- **Taking Responsibility:** Beyond acknowledgment, the individual takes full responsibility for their actions. This involves accepting the consequences of their behavior and understanding that their choices have had an impact on others and the wider community.

- **Making Amends:** Accountability requires the individual to actively engage in actions aimed at making amends for the harm caused. This might involve restitution, restoration, or contributing in meaningful ways to the healing process.

A - ACCOUNTABILITY

- **Self-Reflection and Growth:** The individual is accountable for engaging in self-reflection and personal growth. This includes examining the underlying motivations and triggers that led to their actions and taking steps to address these factors to prevent future harm.

- **Apology and Reconciliation:** Part of accountability involves offering a sincere apology to those affected by their actions. This apology serves as a bridge for reconciliation and demonstrates a genuine commitment to repairing relationships.

- **Commitment to Change:** Accountability encompasses a commitment to changing one's behavior and making choices that align with the values of respect, empathy, and community well-being. This commitment demonstrates a genuine intention to prevent the recurrence of harm.

- **Active Participation:** Throughout the restorative conflict process, the individual is accountable for actively participating in discussions, circles, or meetings. This engagement fosters open communication, facilitates understanding, and promotes healing.

- **Building Trust:** By demonstrating consistent accountability, the individual contributes to rebuilding trust within the community.

A – ACCOUNTABILITY

- Trust is a cornerstone of restorative conflict, and the individual's commitment to accountability helps foster an environment where trust can flourish.

- **Personal Transformation:** True accountability goes beyond surface-level changes. It involves a deep transformation of the individual's mindset, attitudes, and behaviors, leading to personal growth and a redefined relationship with the community.

- **Contributing to Prevention:** Part of the individual's accountability is taking proactive steps to prevent the recurrence of harm. This might involve sharing lessons learned, participating in education, or actively working to prevent similar situations in the future.

In summary, the individual's accountability within the restorative conflict framework embodies a holistic commitment to understanding, healing, transformation, and community well-being. It is a process of active engagement that empowers individuals to take ownership of their actions and contribute to the collective journey toward resolution and growth.

Accountability of the Community

Within the work of restorative conflict, the community assumes a significant mantle of accountability that extends beyond the confines of individual actions. The community's accountability is multifaceted, encompassing responsibilities that contribute to the healing, restoration, and prevention of harm. Central to this accountability is the community's role in creating an environment that nurtures understanding, empathy, and growth. The community is accountable for:

Fostering an atmosphere of inclusion and support.
This entails providing a safe space where all members, whether directly involved in a conflict or not, feel heard and valued. By acknowledging the interconnectedness of individuals within the community, fostering a sense of belonging, and embracing diversity, the community lays a foundation for trust and mutual respect.

A - ACCOUNTABILITY

Promoting open communication and dialogue.

The community's accountability involves facilitating spaces for respectful conversations that encourage participants to share their perspectives, concerns, and hopes. By actively engaging in dialogue, the community helps uncover underlying issues, encourages empathy, and paves the way for the understanding that is essential for conflict resolution.

Supporting healing and reconciliation.

The community's role extends beyond pointing fingers or assigning blame. It involves actively supporting individuals as they navigate the process of healing, both on an individual level and within relationships. By providing resources, guidance, and a collective commitment to growth, the community contributes to the restoration of emotional and social well-being.

Holding individuals accountable collectively.

The community upholds the expectation that individuals acknowledge their actions and make amends, not just for the immediate parties involved, but for the broader community as well. By reinforcing the values of responsibility and integrity, the community promotes a culture of accountability that resonates across its fabric.

In essence, by assuming responsibility for fostering a nurturing environment, facilitating open dialogue, supporting healing, holding individuals accountable, and preventing future harm, the community contributes to the transformative potential of restorative conflict, cultivating a space where conflicts can be addressed with compassion and resolution.

Accountability of Leadership

Leaders have a vital role in building an environment where issues are resolved, and relationships are healed. I've previously discussed the critical role of leadership in creating this kind of positive culture. It's crucial to reiterate that effective leadership is not only about task management and operations; it's equally about possessing the courage to confront personal fears and behaviors, and to learn and grow from that introspection. Without such self-awareness, leaders are at risk of not just failing to resolve issues but potentially exacerbating them. Here, I present four significant errors that leaders, especially those who haven't committed to deep personal reflection, often make. These errors can have a particularly harmful impact on people of color.

Unjust Delegation: The Risk of Overburdening Managers of Color:

This practice places an unfair burden on managers of color, essentially expecting them to take responsibility for issues that aren't theirs to solve just based on a shared racial or ethnic background. It limits the growth opportunities for these managers by bogging them down with disproportionate conflict resolution tasks. Furthermore, it unfairly pigeonholes managers of color as being solely responsible for their peers of color, which can isolate them and detract from their broader leadership roles. It also perpetuates a problematic narrative that racial or ethnic similarities automatically equate to better conflict management, disregarding the individual skills and expertise that each leader brings to the table.

Overlooking Cultural Context in Conflict:
Leaders may fall into the trap of concentrating solely on the individual involved in a conflict, neglecting the broader organizational culture that may have contributed to the issue. By failing to consider how systemic issues or the workplace environment might influence individual crises, leaders miss the opportunity to make comprehensive changes that could prevent similar conflicts in the future.

A - ACCOUNTABILITY

Failure to Model Constructive Behaviors: Leaders are role models in their organizations. When they react to conflicts with defensiveness or aggression rather than with patience and openness to dialogue, they set a negative example. This

can create a workplace culture that mirrors these destructive responses, discouraging open communication and collaboration.

Favoring Quick Fixes Over Real Solutions: Some leaders might opt for the easiest or quickest solution to a conflict, not realizing it doesn't address the root problem. This can lead to recurring issues and diminish trust among team members who feel their concerns are not being taken seriously.

At its heart, the importance of accountability—whether at the individual, community, or leadership level—is about creating a unified approach to healing, growth, and harmony. Each aspect of accountability adds something vital to the overall effort of resolving conflicts. It helps create an environment where people understand each other better, where harm is mended, and relationships are strengthened. Individuals recognizing their faults and changing, communities fostering empathy and preventing further issues, and leaders setting examples and making systemic changes, all combine to form a robust framework. This approach does more than just solve conflicts; it transforms them into chances for meaningful change.

A - ACCOUNTABILITY

This comprehensive approach to accountability is essential for restorative conflict resolution, guiding individuals, communities, and entire organizations towards a collective goal of unity and ongoing improvement.

Reflection Questions:

1. How can you take personal accountability for your actions and contributions to a recent conflict, and what steps can you take to make amends and promote healing?
2. In what ways can your community or organization foster an environment that supports open communication, healing, and accountability?
3. How can leaders within your organization model accountability and foster a culture of trust and constructive conflict resolution?

_____
_____
_____
_____
_____
_____
_____
_____
_____

A - ACCOUNTABILITY

A - ACCOUNTABILITY

C - CHOOSING THE RIGHT PATH FOR REPAIR

Photo by Johannes Plenio on Unsplash

After a disagreement at work, figuring out how to make things right again can be tough. This chapter talks about different ways to help fix those issues and mend relationships. Sometimes, talking to a sounding board can yield good advice. Other times, sitting down just with the person we disagreed with and sorting it out together works best. There are also special methods like restorative coaching, mediation, and circles that guide everyone involved to understand each other better and solve the problem.

C – CHOOSING THE RIGHT PATH FOR REPAIR

Plus, we'll look at how giving and getting feedback the right way can help. Let's explore these paths to see how they can help us move forward, repair relationships, and make things better after conflicts.

Sounding Boards and Informal Venting

Sounding boards serve as invaluable tools in the realm of seeking informal support. In the complexity of our lives, there are moments when we require a space to air our thoughts, test our ideas, or simply vent our emotions. These sounding boards, often consisting of trusted friends, colleagues, or mentors, offer an empathetic ear and a safe place to share our innermost thoughts and feelings. However, it's important to navigate this form of support with care, as even the most well-intentioned discussions can sometimes get complicated.

Using intermediaries to communicate can lead to a problem called triangulation, where messages get twisted as they pass through a third person. This often happens when employees tell their supervisors about a problem but ask them not to tell the other person involved. This ties the supervisor's hands, preventing them from resolving the issue. However, supervisors can also be the ones who cause triangulation by getting too involved. To avoid this, it's important to encourage a workplace culture where people take responsibility for their own emotions and communication.

We should also promote direct discussions between the parties involved, even when those conversations are tough.

It's essential to recognize that, while sounding boards can introduce complexities, they also have their rightful place in certain contexts. Seeking advice or empathy from a sounding board can provide fresh perspectives, alleviate stress, and help us make informed decisions. This practice becomes particularly beneficial when dealing with dilemmas where an objective viewpoint is essential. By setting clear boundaries and emphasizing the importance of confidentiality, we can harness the power of sounding boards to foster personal growth and enhance problem-solving skills, all while minimizing the potential pitfalls associated with triangulation.

Resolving Conflicts 1:1

The 1:1 is a self-resolving conflict model that comes into play when individuals find themselves in disputes that they believe are manageable — conflicts they can handle without outside intervention. In a culture where conflict is normalized, this would be the first recommendation of conflict resolution. This approach is particularly effective in situations where the conflict is not overly complex or emotionally charged, and both parties are willing to engage in open communication.

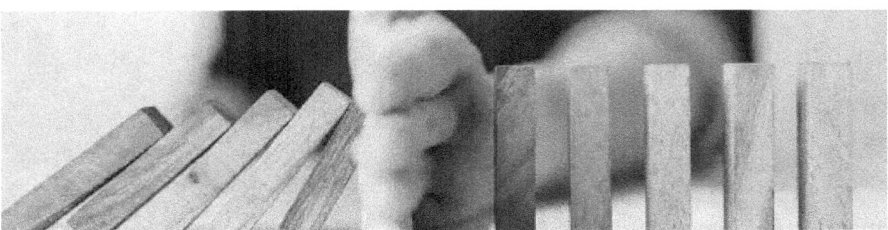

C – CHOOSING THE RIGHT PATH FOR REPAIR

Using the 1:1 resolution model should include these key steps.

1. If applicable, both parties need to understand the organization's restorative conflict model and commit to respectful and constructive dialogue. This means actively listening to each other's perspectives, expressing their own viewpoints, and refraining from blame or personal attacks.

2. A focus on understanding is crucial. This involves asking questions, clarifying misunderstandings, and identifying common ground.

3. Seeking solutions together is important. Brainstorming potential solutions, considering compromises, and finding mutually agreeable outcomes form the heart of this step.

This approach is often considered the best way to resolve conflicts for several reasons. It empowers individuals by giving them agency over the resolution process. It preserves relationships by fostering open communication and understanding. Additionally, self-resolving conflicts tend to be resolved more quickly and with less negative emotional impact, allowing individuals to move forward.

However, it's important to note that not all conflicts are suited for this approach, especially when power dynamics are imbalanced, emotions run high, or when specialized expertise is required. In such cases, seeking assistance from a mediator or other conflict resolution professional might be more appropriate.

Following is a guide to get you started...

Invite them to engage in a restorative conversation keeping the invitation light, using "I" statements. Let them decide the time and place:

"I wanted to check in with you about _____ because (why it's important to you) and I want to restore anything that may be off. Is now a good time, or would you prefer to schedule a more convenient time for us to chat?"

Acknowledge their willingness to participate:

"Hey [Name], I really appreciate you taking the time to talk. I know you're busy."

C – CHOOSING THE RIGHT PATH FOR REPAIR

Clearly express intent and concerns:

"I want to start by saying that I value our relationship and the time we've spent working on this team/project together. Lately, I've been feeling a bit uneasy about something, and I thought it would be best to discuss it openly."

Using "I" Statements and descriptive words (I noticed, I saw, I heard):

"I've noticed that [describe the behavior or situation you're concerned about]. It's been affecting me in a way that I wanted to share with you."

Describing Feelings and Perspective:

"When [describe the behavior or situation], I feel [describe your emotions, such as hurt, frustrated, embarrassed, etc.]. You probably don't even realize it. I'm just sharing so we can be aligned and talk about how we can support each other and work through this together."

Acknowledging Your Role

Before we go any further, I want to acknowledge that I understand my own role in this. Looking back, I realize that there might have been times when did/said the same thing. I didn't let you know how I felt, or wasn't clear, and that could have contributed to the situation.

Encouraging Their Perspective

"Is this making sense? I'd really appreciate hearing your thoughts on this." "How do you see the situation?" "I want to understand your perspective better." [PLEASE remember to use active listening and responding with nodding and verbal cues like "Oh I see," "I can totally understand how that would feel," "Yep! I would be embarrassed too."

Finding Common Ground

"It clear that we both care about [mention a shared value or goal]. I think that's a great starting point for us to work through this." Or "I think we just got sidetracked with…"

"It clear that we both care about [mention a shared value or goal]. I think that's a great starting point for us to work through this." Or "I think we just got sidetracked with…"

Action Steps

"I love the solutions we came up with. How about we commit to trying [mention one or two actionable steps] over the next [mention a timeframe] and then reconvene to see how things are going?"

Expressing Gratitude and Reaffirming Relationship

"Phew I feel so much better, thank you!" "I'm glad we had this conversation." "It means a lot to me that we can talk openly about things that matter." "I believe this will help us." "What about you? Are you good?"

Restorative 1:1 Coaching

Unlike a typical executive coach who focuses on individual achievement, a restorative coach focuses on the interconnectedness of individuals within their communities. Restorative Coaching places emphasis on understanding how personal narratives, relationships, and experiences shape behavior, fostering self-awareness and empathy. Through thoughtful conversations, restorative coaching encourages individuals to explore the impact of their actions on others, *promoting accountability* and a commitment to making amends when harm has occurred. This unique coaching style aims not only for personal success but also for the harmonious coexistence of individuals in their broader contexts.

Some organizations choose to select and train staff members to assume roles as coaches. The benefit of this model is that not only have staff members been trained to support their teammates, but in doing so they are also internalizing and leading the very values of a restorative culture that are being implemented. Ideally, the more staff members who become coaches the sooner the organization transforms. The downside is that coaching is a technical skill, however it is also an instinctive skill that takes courage to name things that may not be easy for the person being coached to hear. It also requires the finesse to know when/if people are ready to hear it or not.

Additionally, restorative coaching engages participants in an active process of reflection, dialogue, and action. It creates a safe space for individuals to explore their stories, uncover underlying motives, and identify opportunities for growth. By recognizing the ripple effects of their behavior, individuals are empowered to make intentional choices that align with their values and contribute positively to their communities. Restorative coaching, thus, serves as a bridge between personal development and collective well-being.

Restorative Mediation

Restorative mediation is an effective method for resolving conflicts between two or more individuals in the workplace.

C – CHOOSING THE RIGHT PATH FOR REPAIR

As a facilitator, the goal is to provide a neutral and structured process that allows participants to express their concerns, needs, and emotions in a safe and controlled environment.

Here is a process I use:

1. The facilitator meets with each party separately to understand each one's perspectives and goals for mediation.
2. The facilitator then brings the parties together and guides the conversation, ensuring that everyone has an opportunity to speak and be heard. The facilitator encourages active listening and promotes empathy by encouraging participants to reflect on the impact of their actions on others.
3. The facilitator then helps the parties identify common interests, explore potential solutions, and, if resolution isn't possible, helps parties develop a *conflict management* plan to move forward.

Restorative mediation fosters ownership, accountability, and the restoration of relationships, enabling individuals to move forward and collaborate more effectively. The timeline for mediation will vary depending on the conflict and who is involved.

Once individuals have agreed to participate in restorative mediation, the coach or coaches facilitating in the mediation will seek to add individual meetings and joint meetings to the calendar as soon as reasonably possible. If one or more participants have significant scheduling conflicts, the coach will work with the employee to prioritize the mediation process and identify times when they can commit to participating.

Restorative Circles

In workplaces, there are times when the restorative culture gets tested. That's when the idea of using restorative circles comes into play. Circles are different in that they are like structured conversations where people come together to talk openly and understand each other better.

They're especially helpful when there's been an ongoing problem that's been making the team more tense, when something big happens that affects a lot of people, or when a few people are part of something that others witness and cause indirect harm. These restorative circles are invaluable as they give everyone a chance to talk, be heard, listen, and heal. This serves as a kind of "reset" for teams or individuals to move forward without the baggage and mitigates the inevitable erosion that occurs when people bottle things up.

Following is an example of how I lead my restorative circles:

Step 1: Preparation

Identify Participants: Determine who should participate in the circle. This might include the victim, offender, and any supporters or community members.

Select a Facilitator: Choose a trained facilitator who is neutral and skilled in guiding a restorative conflict healing circle/process.

Choose a Safe Space: Find a comfortable, neutral and distraction-free location where all participants can sit in a circle, promoting an atmosphere of equality and open communication.

Step 2: Opening/ Tone-setting

Welcome and Introductions: The facilitator welcomes everyone and introduces the purpose of the circle, emphasizing the principles of grace, dignity, listening, and understanding.

Establish Guidelines: Establish ground rules for the conversation, including speaking one at a time, active listening, and maintaining confidentiality.

Step 3: Sharing Stories (Skilled Facilitation Needed)

Person who was harmed shares their story: The person who was harmed starts by sharing their experience, feelings, and the impact of the harm. They express in terms of their emotions, fears, and needs.

Person who caused harm shares: The person who caused harm shares their perspective, taking responsibility for their actions. This might include explanations, feelings, missteps, *intentions*, remorse. (Yes, intentions. It helps the person harmed to understand the full context of the incident, which can be vital for healing. Additionally, expressing the original intentions can differentiate between deliberate harm and a misunderstanding or mistake, which can influence the path towards reconciliation and trust-building.)

Others' Perspectives: If supporters or community members are present, they may also share their thoughts and feelings about the situation. This is not so much about centering their experiences, more so, to witness and support the healing process.

Step 4: Open Dialogue (Skilled Facilitation Needed)

Facilitated Questions: The facilitator asks open-ended questions that encourage participants to share, empathize, and understand each other's viewpoints. These questions might include, "How has this situation affected you?" or "What needs to happen for healing to occur?"

Responses: Participants take turns responding to the questions while holding the talking piece. The focus is on active listening and understanding rather than immediate resolution.

Step 5: Reaching Agreements

Generating Ideas: The group discusses potential actions or agreements that could help repair the harm and address the needs of everyone involved.

Consensus: Participants work together to reach a consensus on the agreements, considering the harmed person's needs for restoration and the accountability of the person who caused the harm.

Step 6: Closing

Appreciation: Each participant shares an appreciation for the process and the opportunity to speak and listen.

Closure: The facilitator concludes the circle, reiterating the agreements reached and acknowledging the commitment made by everyone.

Step 7: Follow-Up

Implementation: The agreements reached during the circle are put into action. This might involve the offender fulfilling certain obligations or making amends.

Continued Support: Depending on the outcome, nature of the harm, and the agreements, participants might continue to receive support, counseling, or follow-up circles.

Remember, restorative circles can change to fit different situations and cultures. The aim is to build understanding, help heal, and get people to take responsibility by talking things out and making agreements together. It's important to have someone trained leading the circle and to keep everyone safe and supported during it.

Restorative Feedback/ Performance Management

Receiving feedback is a fundamental aspect of personal and professional growth, yet it is a process that many individuals struggle with in the workplace. Feedback, whether positive or constructive, often triggers a range of emotions and challenges our sense of self-worth and competence. People may find it difficult to accept feedback due to fear of judgment, a desire to protect their self-image, or a lack of trust in the intentions of the feedback giver.

Additionally, the way feedback is delivered and the overall culture surrounding feedback within the organization can heavily influence how individuals perceive and respond to it. Understanding the underlying reasons why people struggle with feedback is essential for fostering a more constructive feedback culture that encourages learning, development, and collaboration in the workplace.

The power of restorative feedback lies in its ability to create an environment of trust, growth, and collaboration in the workplace. Unlike traditional feedback approaches that often focus solely on pointing out flaws or deficiencies, restorative feedback takes a holistic view of individuals, considering their strengths, accomplishments, and potential for development. By emphasizing open and honest communication, restorative feedback fosters a sense of psychological safety, allowing individuals to be more receptive to feedback and to view it as an opportunity for growth rather than criticism. Restorative feedback encourages dialogue, active listening, and mutual understanding, enabling both the feedback giver and receiver to engage in a collaborative process of learning, reflection, and improvement.

C – CHOOSING THE RIGHT PATH OF REPAIR

This approach builds stronger relationships, promotes self-awareness, and empowers individuals to take ownership of their development, ultimately contributing to a positive and thriving work environment.

A sample of a restorative feedback conversation

"Sarah, I want to acknowledge the excellent work you've done on the recent project. Your attention to detail, problem-solving skills, and dedication have been instrumental in achieving the project's success. Your ability to collaborate with the team and adapt to changing circumstances has been impressive. I appreciate your initiative and the positive impact you've made on the overall team dynamics. On a scale from 1 to 10, I'd give you an 8. Now, I want to offer you some feedback that can take you to a 10.

During the project, there were a few instances where your communication with stakeholders could have been more proactive and transparent. For example, when it became clear that you wouldn't get the report to Tom on time, you should have told him then so that he could plan accordingly. I understand that managing so many moving parts can be challenging but providing timely updates helps us all stay on the same page. By strengthening this aspect of your communication, you will further enhance your effectiveness in driving successful outcomes and maintaining strong working relationships.

"I would love your feedback on this as well, and if you need any support or guidance with any of these recommendations, you know I've got your back. My number one goal *and responsibility* is to make sure you are growing and developing in this role where your strengths are maximized, and our team is stronger. Is there anything you'd like to share about the feedback or need more support on? Is there any context I may be missing? Is there anything in general? How do you feel?"

In Summary: Backstage Secrets to a Stellar Performance Review

- Kick things off by letting them know they're already hitting some high notes like a true rockstar.

- Detail the specific moves that could turn their solid performance into an unforgettable showstopper.

- Show how their solo act can turn up the volume on the team's harmony and get everyone cheering.

C – CHOOSING THE RIGHT PATH OF REPAIR

- Offer them an all-access pass to your support and mentorship—let them know you're their number one fan.

- Flip the script and invite them to jam in the conversation, tuning into their side of the story.

- Make sure the feedback sets the stage for an epic comeback, with a follow-up gig to celebrate the wins and plan the next chart-topper.

In conclusion, restorative feedback holds tremendous potential for transforming the way we approach performance management and personal development in the workplace. By embracing restorative feedback in our performance management processes, we can shift the focus from blame and criticism to growth and collaboration. Restorative feedback fosters a culture of trust, openness, and mutual respect, allowing individuals to learn from their experiences, acknowledge their strengths, and address areas for improvement. *But most of all, it normalizes feedback as part of the culture where people no longer dread being evaluated.*

Conflict Management v. Conflict Resolution

In some cases, people cross paths with others they are destined to clash with. No matter the efforts expended, or the strategies employed, our differences persist, refusing to find a harmonious meeting point. These challenging junctures where we find ourselves at the crossroads of understanding, we must acknowledge that, sometimes, some people just don't get along.

In these instances, we turn our attention to Conflict *Management* as *resolution* is not an option in the moment. Conflict Management is a process designed to navigate disagreements, ensuring that, even during irreconcilable differences, we can still find ways to coexist and collaborate. The aim of conflict management isn't to force an immediate agreement but rather to ensure that disagreements don't escalate into destructive conflict.

One of my clients had two team members who simply could not get along. They were valued on the team and performed excellent work. The team as a whole was great, and everyone got along well except for these two individuals, and everyone knew it.

Part of our conflict management strategy was to shift assignments that involved them interrelating. One of them opted to work remotely, which they had planned to do six months later — we just implemented that arrangement sooner. In other situations, people may end up moving into different departments. Just know that irreconcilable conflicts between members don't just affect the individuals involved. Others feel the indirect stress and tension, so it's better to figure out how to manage conflicts sooner rather than later.

C – CHOOSING THE RIGHT PATH FOR REPAIR

Reflection Questions:

1. When faced with a conflict at work, how can you determine the most appropriate method for resolution—whether it be through informal venting, a direct 1:1 conversation, or more structured approaches like restorative coaching, mediation, or circles?
2. How can you use the principles of restorative feedback to provide constructive and empathetic feedback to your colleagues, promoting growth and maintaining positive relationships?
3. Reflect on a recent conflict you experienced. How could you have applied the steps of a 1:1 restorative conversation to address the issue more effectively? What specific changes in your approach might have led to a better outcome?

C – CHOOSING THE RIGHT PATH FOR REPAIR

C – CHOOSING THE RIGHT PATH FOR REPAIR

Photo by Chirstina @ wocintechchate.com on Unsplash

E - EVALUATE AND EVOLVE

The journey towards being an environment that can powerfully manage conflict is not a one-time achievement but a fluid process that demands constant reevaluation and development.

Assessment is a vital step on this path. It involves a regular examination of your organization's approach to handling conflicts, pinpointing areas for improvement, and evaluating the emotional well-being of the team. This reflective practice not only highlights what is currently effective but also shines a light on opportunities for positive change.

E – EVALUATE AND EVOLVE

An example of a conflict management assessment that your organization could use to evaluate its approach to handling conflict could be a survey. Here is a sample to give you some ideas:

Section 1: Conflict Identification and Frequency

1. **How often do conflicts arise in your team/department?**
   - Never
   - Rarely
   - Occasionally
   - Frequently
   - Very Frequently

2. **What are the most common sources of conflict in your workplace? (Check all that apply)**

   ◊ Communication breakdowns
   ◊ Role ambiguity
   ◊ Workload distribution
   ◊ Interpersonal issues
   ◊ Differences in values or priorities
   ◊ Resource allocation

E – EVALUATE AND EVOLVE

Section 2: Conflict Resolution Processes

3. How effective are the current conflict resolution processes in your organization?

    - Very Ineffective
    - Ineffective
    - Neutral
    - Effective
    - Very Effective

4. Which conflict resolution methods are currently used in your organization? (Check all that apply)

    - Informal discussions
    - Mediation
    - Restorative circles
    - Formal grievance procedures
    - External consultants

5. How accessible are conflict resolution resources and support for employees?

    - Not Accessible
    - Somewhat Accessible
    - Neutral
    - Accessible
    - Very Accessible

E – EVALUATE AND EVOLVE

Section 3: Training and Development

6. Have you received training on conflict resolution in the past year?
   - Yes
   - No

7. How confident do you feel in your ability to manage conflicts effectively?
   - Not Confident
   - Somewhat Confident
   - Neutral
   - Confident
   - Very Confident

8. What additional training or resources would help you better manage conflicts? (Open-ended)

Section 4: Emotional Well-Being and Organizational Culture

9. How would you rate the overall emotional well-being of your team?
   - Very Poor
   - Poor
   - Neutral
   - Good
   - Very Good

E – EVALUATE AND EVOLVE

10. How supportive is the organizational culture in promoting open communication and conflict resolution?

    - Not Supportive
    - Somewhat Supportive
    - Neutral
    - Supportive
    - Very Supportive

11. What changes could improve the emotional well-being of the team and the effectiveness of conflict management? (Open-ended)

Section 5: Outcomes and Continuous Improvement

12. Have past conflicts typically resulted in positive outcomes and strengthened relationships?

    - Never
    - Rarely
    - Sometimes
    - Often
    - Always

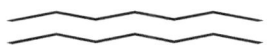

E – EVALUATE AND EVOLVE

13. How regularly does your team reflect on and learn from resolved conflicts?

    - Never
    - Rarely
    - Sometimes
    - Often
    - Always

14. What specific actions can be taken to enhance the evaluation and evolution of conflict management practices in your organization? (Open-ended)

Implementation and Analysis

- **Distribute the Survey:** Share the assessment survey with all team members, ensuring anonymity to encourage honest feedback.

- **Collect and Analyze Data:** Compile the responses and analyze the data to identify common themes, strengths, and areas needing improvement.

- **Develop Action Plans:** Based on the assessment results, create action plans to address identified issues, such as providing additional training, improving access to conflict resolution resources, or enhancing communication channels.

E – EVALUATE AND EVOLVE

- **Monitor Progress:** Regularly revisit the assessment to monitor progress, make necessary adjustments, and ensure continuous improvement in conflict management practices.

Following assessment is the necessity to evolve. This phase is about leveraging the insights gained to bolster and refine your workplace.

It is about perceiving each resolved conflict as an opportunity for learning and growth. Adopting this perspective transforms the workplace, allowing it not just to cope with disputes but to utilize them as a driving force for innovation and team solidarity.

A workplace committed to this cycle of evaluation and evolution understands that the ability to manage conflict comes from an eagerness to adapt and improve continuously. It is an ongoing commitment to self-reflection and action that not only mitigates confrontations but also propels the organization towards a culture of mutual understanding, productivity, and unity. Such a workplace does not merely endure conflicts but uses them as steppingstones to reinforce solidarity and cooperation with every challenge faced.

E – EVALUATE AND EVOLVE

This chapter serves as a call to action for leaders and employees alike to maintain a vigilant and forward-thinking approach. It's about striving not just for conflict resolution but for a state of constant progression and

betterment. Here, in the rhythm of evaluation and evolution, the groundwork for enduring collaboration and workplace harmony is established.

E – EVALUATE AND EVOLVE

Reflection Questions:

1. How can your organization implement a regular and effective conflict management assessment process to identify areas of improvement and ensure continuous development?
2. In what ways can viewing each resolved conflict as an opportunity for learning and growth transform your organization's approach to handling disputes? How can this perspective be fostered among team members?
3. Can you recall a recent conflict resolution in your workplace? What lessons were learned from that experience, and how can these insights be applied to refine future approaches to conflict?

E – EVALUATE AND EVOLVE

REAL STORIES, REAL RESOLUTIONS

In this chapter, we delve into the story of Tom, a dedicated attorney whose longstanding commitment to Majors Legal Aid Services has been marked by excellence and a deeply personal approach to legal aid. As the organization embarks on a crucial transformation toward more inclusive and equitable practices, Tom finds himself at a crossroads, grappling with the shift from his established methods to the new demands of accountability and transparency. This narrative explores the challenges of adapting to change within a professional setting and the complex dynamics between tradition and progress.

Tom's Struggles: Navigating Change and Commitment at Majors Legal Aid Services

For over three decades, Tom has been an integral part of Majors Legal Aid Services. A sharp, dedicated civil legal aid attorney, Tom is a white male in his late 60s, well-loved and highly respected in the communities he serves and by his coworkers. Known for his hard work and effective methods, Tom has built his career on a foundation of autonomy and established personal routines that have served both him and his clients well.

Recently, Majors Legal Aid Services has embarked on a transformative journey to ensure that all policies, practices, and cultural norms are aligned with principles of equity and transparency. This initiative has been embraced organization-wide, with all staff members participating in the newly implemented equity trainings— all, except Tom.

Historically, Tom has not been one to attend many meetings, preferring to focus intensely on his casework. This hands-off approach has never been questioned until now, as the new DEI efforts call for greater accountability and transparency from everyone. These changes, though well-intentioned, have brought Tom considerable frustration. The concept of being "micromanaged" in the name of equity grates on him, leading to the question: "Why now? Why can't I just do my work?"

The Executive Director, Michael, while deeply committed to the transformative DEI initiatives, felt mounting pressure and frustration due to Tom's reluctance to engage with the new organizational norms. This frustration was compounded by increasing discontent among other staff members, some of whom felt it was unjust that Tom was allowed to opt out of the DEI work. Voices within the team argued that Tom should either be forced to participate or be let go, asserting that the validity of the entire DEI effort was compromised if participation was optional. Managing this internal conflict and balancing the divergent views within the team proved to be one of the most challenging aspects of Michael's role. Michael recognized the necessity of balancing firm leadership with empathetic understanding, especially given Tom's longstanding contribution to the organization. This delicate balancing act required affirming Tom's invaluable legacy while steering him and the entire team towards embracing change, making their role immensely demanding yet crucial for the organization's progress. This scenario underscored the delicate nature of leadership during times of significant cultural shifts within an organization.

The sentiment among staff toward the DEI initiatives was now mixed and charged with emotion. While many embraced the change, seeing it as a crucial step towards a more equitable workplace, others were disenchanted, particularly with the inconsistency in participation.

The exemption of Tom, a longstanding and respected member, from these initiatives sparked a significant divide. Some staff members felt it created a double standard that undermined the integrity of the efforts, leading to feelings of frustration and disillusionment. They argued that true equity meant universal participation, without exceptions. This tension highlighted the challenges of implementing systemic changes within an established organization and underscored the need for transparent, inclusive decision-making processes that could accommodate and address the diverse perspectives within the team.

The situation escalated when Michael approached Tom to discuss the importance of his engagement in these organizational efforts, including the new requirement for all staff to enter their hours into the Legal Server system. This confrontation led to a conflict that highlighted underlying tensions related to change, generational differences, and the nature of DEI work itself.

Navigating the Generational Divide

Tom represents a generation traditionally characterized by a strong work ethic and a preference for independence over oversight. Many in his age group might view constant meetings and formalized reporting as bureaucratic red tape that hinders their real work. On the other hand, the younger workforce tends to value transparency and collective action, often welcoming structured approaches like DEI initiatives that emphasize systemic change and accountability.

This divergence in workplace values often leads to friction as traditional methods clash with progressive approaches. While Tom may perceive these new practices as an unnecessary complication of his tried-and-true routines, the younger generation sees them as vital tools to ensure fairness and equity within the organization. Bridging this gap requires a dialogue that respects the merits of both perspectives. By fostering an understanding that views these DEI efforts not as hurdles but as enhancements to the foundational work laid by experienced professionals like Tom, the organization can create a more cohesive and supportive environment. Such discussions can lead to innovative solutions that honor past contributions while embracing the necessary evolution of practices that meet contemporary standards of equity and inclusion.

Resolutions and Conversations

Affirm Tom's Legacy and Contributions: Senior staff like Tom often feel unseen by younger staff and perhaps even obsolete, which can heighten resistance to new initiatives. Coming from a place of grace, it becomes important to affirm the value of every generation's contributions. It's crucial for the Executive Director to affirm Tom's legacy and the impact of his work at Majors Legal Aid Services.

REAL STORIES, REAL RESOLUTIONS

This can be accomplished through public acknowledgements at meetings, feature stories in organizational newsletters, or special recognition events. By celebrating his contributions, the organization not only honors Tom but also reinforces the value of his dedication and expertise, underscoring that these new DEI initiatives are built upon the strong foundation laid by seasoned professionals like him. This recognition can help Tom feel a continued sense of belonging and appreciation, potentially easing his transition into the new organizational norms.

Personalize Discussions: The ED could schedule a one-on-one meeting with Tom in a neutral, comfortable setting. Begin by acknowledging Tom's invaluable contributions over the years, emphasizing his respected status. Transition into a discussion on how the landscape of legal aid is evolving and how inclusivity and accountability are becoming essential components of service.

Explore Underlying Needs and Emotions: Explore Underlying Needs and Emotions: It's important to address the possibility that Tom's anger might be a surface expression of deeper feelings such as embarrassment or shame due to perceived changes in his capabilities or relevance. Additionally, financial concerns or an illness might be influencing his decision to remain at the job, adding layers of complexity to his situation.

The Executive Director should facilitate a safe space for deeper, more personal conversations that allow Tom to express these vulnerabilities without fear of judgment.

By understanding the root causes of Tom's discomfort, including any personal challenges he might be facing, the organization can better support him in adapting to new norms while respecting his feelings and dignity.

Be Flexible and Compromise: Recognize Tom's need for autonomy and propose a compromise where he can have flexibility in some areas, provided he meets the key transparency requirements like logging hours.

Mentorship Role: Encourage Tom to view his engagement in these initiatives as an opportunity to mentor younger attorneys and staff, passing on his knowledge while learning from the fresh perspectives they bring.

The Realities of DEI Work

As DEI efforts deepen, it's not uncommon for some staff to feel alienated, leading to departures. This can be particularly true for long-standing members like Tom who may find the new culture challenging to adapt to. It's essential for Michael to prepare for this possibility, ensuring that the transition is handled with grace and understanding.

If possible, always provide as much runway as feasible for the staff member to adjust to their departure.

In the event that someone chooses to leave, it is important to support those who choose to stay through continuous engagement and personalized support while also respecting the decisions of those who may choose to leave. By doing so, the organization can manage changes thoughtfully, minimizing disruptions and fostering a culture of inclusivity and respect for everyone's journey.

In navigating these complex dynamics, the overarching goal is to foster an environment where every staff member feels valued, seen, and heard, contributing to a genuinely inclusive and equitable workplace.

RESOLUTION

As the DEI initiatives at Majors Legal Aid Services unfolded, Michael, and a skilled Restorative Conflict Specialist, faced a delicate situation with Tom, as a longstanding attorney resistant to the new changes. Understanding the depth of Tom's unease and the broader staff concerns about equity, Michael approached the situation with a nuanced strategy of engagement and empathy.

After several personal discussions with Tom, it became clear that despite best efforts, Tom felt that the new direction of the organization no longer aligned with his personal and professional desires.

Recognizing the importance of preserving Tom's dignity, the staff trust, and the organization's integrity, Michael worked closely with Tom to plan a respectful and gradual exit that honored his decades of service.

Michael arranged for a series of celebratory events highlighting Tom's contributions, coupled with a comprehensive retirement plan that provided Tom with security and acknowledgment. He also initiated a knowledge transfer period, during which Tom could mentor selected attorneys, passing on his invaluable expertise, ensuring his legacy would continue to influence the organization.

The staff were kept informed throughout the process, ensuring transparency and inclusivity. Michael's leadership reaffirmed the staff's trust in the fairness of the DEI initiatives, proving that even challenging transitions could be managed with grace and respect. Tom's departure was marked by a sense of communal respect and gratitude, illustrating how thoughtful leadership can facilitate even the most difficult changes with dignity and foresight.

CONCLUSION

"You Can't Heal What You Won't Reveal."

In conclusion, the power of healing and restoration in the workplace through restorative conflict practices cannot be understated. By embracing a restorative approach, organizations have the opportunity to transform conflicts into learning experiences, repair relationships, and create cultures of trust, empathy, and accountability. Restorative conflict offers a path to address harm and conflicts in a way that promotes understanding, growth, and healing for all individuals involved.

We must recognize that conflicts and power imbalances exist in every workplace; it is our collective responsibility to address them in a restorative manner. The call to action is clear: let us commit ourselves to creating workplaces where restorative conflict principles and practices are embedded in our policies, procedures, and everyday interactions. This requires ongoing education, communication, and leadership support to foster a culture that values dialogue, collaboration, and the well-being of individuals.

CONCLUSION

Let's harness the power of restorative conflict to create workplaces that are truly anchored in fairness, respect, and compassion. It's with this dedication that we can forge lasting change, not just in our workplaces, but in the fabric of our society, cultivating a legacy of unity and collective well-being.

As we conclude our exploration of restorative conflict practices, it becomes clear that transforming workplace conflicts into opportunities for growth and healing is not just a possibility—it's a necessity for fostering a culture of trust, empathy, and accountability. At Majors Leadership Group, we specialize in guiding organizations through this transformative journey.

Why Choose Majors Leadership Group?

With years of experience in conflict resolution and leadership development, our team at Majors Leadership Group is uniquely equipped to help your organization navigate the complexities of workplace conflicts. We understand the nuances of different organizational cultures and tailor our approach to meet your specific needs.

CONCLUSION

We don't believe in one-size-fits-all solutions. Our services are customized to address the unique challenges and dynamics of your workplace. Whether through restorative coaching, mediation, training workshops, or policy development, we provide comprehensive strategies that align with your organizational goals.

Our clients have experienced significant improvements in their workplace environments, including increased trust, improved communication, and stronger team cohesion. We have helped organizations of all sizes turn conflicts into catalysts for positive change.

At Majors Leadership Group, we don't just address immediate conflicts; we equip your organization with the tools and skills needed to handle future challenges effectively.

Here are the questions Dr. Majors will help you answer:

1. How can you start integrating restorative conflict principles into your organization's policies and daily interactions to promote a culture of trust, empathy, and accountability?
2. What specific steps can your organization take to provide ongoing education and support for employees and leaders to effectively engage in restorative conflict resolution?
3. Reflect on a recent conflict in your workplace. How could a restorative approach have changed the outcome, and what can you do differently in the future to apply these principles?

CONCLUSION

Now is the time to take the first step towards creating a more harmonious and productive workplace. By partnering with Majors Leadership Group, you will gain a trusted ally in your journey towards a culture of fairness, respect, and compassion. Let us help you harness the power of restorative conflict to build a stronger, more resilient organization.

Don't wait for conflicts to escalate. Contact Majors Leadership Group today to learn how we can support your organization's growth and well-being. Together, we can transform your workplace into a thriving environment where every individual feels valued and heard.

Contact Dr. Majors:
info@MajorsLeadership.com
www.MajorsLeadership.com

Empower your organization with the expertise and guidance of Majors Leadership Group. Because the journey to a better workplace starts with a single call.

REFERENCES

Edmondson, A. (1999). Psychological safety and learning behavior in work teams. Administrative Science Quarterly, 44(2), 350-383.

Carmeli, A., Brueller, D., & Dutton, J. E. (2009). Learning behaviors in the workplace: The role of high-quality interpersonal relationships and psychological safety. Systems Research and Behavioral Science, 26(1), 81-98.

Gottman, J. M., & Silver, N. (1999). The Seven Principles for Making Marriage Work. Crown Publishers.

Decety, J., & Cowell, J. M. (2014). The complex relation between morality and empathy. Trends in Cognitive Sciences, 18(7), 337-339.

Deutsch, M., & Coleman, P. T. (Eds.). (2000). The Handbook of Conflict Resolution: Theory and Practice. Jossey-Bass.

Braithwaite, J. (2002). Restorative Justice and Responsive Regulation. Oxford University Press.

Zehr, H. (2002). The Little Book of Restorative Justice. Good Books.

Dweck, C. S. (2006). Mindset: The New Psychology of Success. Random House.

Thank you for reading my book!

If you want to talk more about these ideas or see what else I'm up to, I'd love to hear from you. Check out these places where we can keep in touch:

- Instagram.com/@MajorsLeadership
- Facebook.com/@MajorsLeadership
- https://www.linkedin.com/in/majorsleadership/
- Youtube.com/@MajorsLeadership
- Website: www.MajorsLeadership.com

www.MajorsLeadership.com

© 2024 Majors Leadership Group. All right reserved

www.ingramcontent.com/pod-product-compliance
Lightning Source LLC
Chambersburg PA
CBHW070142230526
45471CB00002B/476